15.95

FOOD
THROUGH THE AGES

PIERO VENTURA

SIMON & SCHUSTER
YOUNG BOOKS

First published in Great Britain in 1994 by
Simon & Schuster Young Books
Campus 400
Maylands Avenue
Hemel Hempstead
Herts HP2 7EZ

© 1993 Arnoldo Mondadori Editore S.p.A. Milan

Prepared with the assistance of
Max Casalini, Marisa Murgo Ventura, Pierluigi Longo
and Massimo Messina

English text © 1994 Simon & Schuster Young Books

ISBN 0 7500 1576 4

A catalogue record for this book is available from the British Library

Printed in Spain by Artes Gráficas Toledo, S.A.
D.L.TO:389-1994

CONTENTS

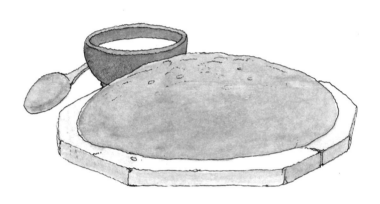

Introduction	4	Food from the New World	34
Hunting and gathering	5	Maize and potatoes	36
Weapons for hunting	6	New technology	38
Early fishing	8	The American prairie	40
Domesticating animals	10	Steam engines on the farm	42
The first farmers	12	Freezing and chilling	44
Farming in Ancient Egypt	14	Canning food	46
Feeding imperial Rome	16	Intensive farming	48
Inside a Roman farm	18	Breeding livestock	50
Bread	20	The dairy industry	52
The grain trade	22	A balanced diet	54
Markets, shops and streetsellers	25	Modern conservation methods	56
Smallholdings and monastery farms	26	Factory fishing	58
The mill and the plough	28	Food in the future	60
Spices, salt and honey	30	Glossary	62
Plague and plenty	32	Index	64

INTRODUCTION

In prehistoric times people spent most of their time searching for food. They were hunter-gatherers, killing animals for meat and picking up nuts, berries and plants where they could. They ate what they could find. Today we can choose from a huge variety of food which we buy at shops and supermarkets. Food is now an industry.

How and when did this happen?
The most important change came after about 8000 BC, when people learned to how to cultivate wheat and barley and to tame wild sheep, cattle and goats. Over the centuries since then, people have developed new ways to grow more food more efficiently and breed better animals.

Food has also shaped history. Society and civilization only became possible when people settled in one place to grow crops. Great empires expanded, partly because they needed to find more food to feed their huge populations. Explorers looking for new routes for the spice trade discovered the New World. Small countries such as Holland and England became mighty sea powers for a time because of the sailing skills developed by their fishermen.

This book tells the story of food. It describes the different ways people grew crops and raised animals, the tools and techniques they invented to help them, how they used the technology of their times to preserve food so that it could be stored or transported, and how the search for food has affected the history of the world.

HUNTING AND GATHERING

Finding and catching

Until about 12,000 years ago, no-one lived in one settled place. People were always looking for food, and so they had to move about the country. The earliest humans relied on finding roots, nuts, berries, fruit and other plant food and small or slow-moving animals such as lizards, turtles, grubs and insects. They also took the meat left over when a lion or tiger had killed a large animal such as a buffalo or a rhinoceros. They learned to catch small animals either by throwing rocks at them or by digging holes to trap them.

Learning to hunt

Gradually, people learned more about how to kill large animals and provide a longer-lasting supply of food. They learned how to creep up on animals and catch them unawares. They learned to chase large animals over a high crag so that they would hurt themselves and be easier to kill. The American Plains Indians used this trick to hunt buffalo as late as the 18th century (1700–1800). People also learned how to track herds of animals as they moved to new grazing land, how to hunt together in a group and how to make and use weapons.

WEAPONS FOR HUNTING

In for the kill

The first hunting weapons were light as they were made from horn or bone. They were only useful for killing small or weak animals. Later on, spears and arrow heads were made from flint or stone and were more powerful. People used these weapons to attack animals bigger than themselves and to fight off the lions, tigers and hyenas that were also hunting for food.

Using spears and bows and arrows, people could hunt at a distance from the animals with less risk of getting hurt themselves. Bows and arrows were especially useful, as each hunter carried several arrows and so could make more than one shot at the prey. By working together as a group, the hunters had much more chance of hitting the target. They could kill several animals at a time to provide enough meat for the whole tribe.

Bringing home the bacon

Using their flint knives, the hunters could skin and cut up large animals where they were killed to make it easier to take them back to the home camp. Sometimes they would drag the animal to a 'kill site', a special cave or secret place near the hunting ground. Here they could cut up the carcase without wolves bothering them.

Mammoths, bison and oxen were favourite prey animals as they were very large and provided food for a lot of people. There was about 1 000 Kg of meat on a boned mammoth.

Early hunters may have discovered cold storage. If there was too much meat to take back all at once, it was probably left at the kill site to be collected later. Icy weather chilled the meat and people would have noticed that meat left in the cold lasted longer than meat kept in a warm cave.

The first weapons

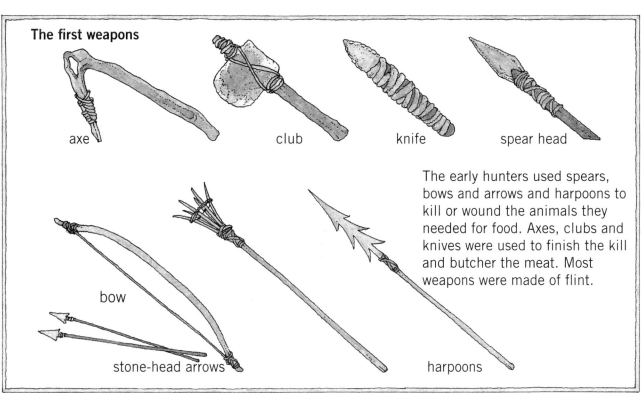

axe   club   knife   spear head

The early hunters used spears, bows and arrows and harpoons to kill or wound the animals they needed for food. Axes, clubs and knives were used to finish the kill and butcher the meat. Most weapons were made of flint.

bow

stone-head arrows   harpoons

EARLY FISHING

Before reliable boats were made, people fished from the safety of the riverbank or in the shallows. They used clubs and spears. Everybody went fishing, including young children and old people.

Fishing for all

As well as hunting for meat and gathering fruit and plant food, people caught fish to eat. If they lived near the coast, they picked up crabs, mussels and shellfish from the beach. As they followed the grazing herds of mammoth or reindeer, they crossed over rivers and streams where they caught freshwater fish.

Only the fittest and strongest people, usually men, went hunting. The women concentrated on looking for plant food and small animals, which kept the tribe going when the hunt was not successful or when large animals were scarce. But everybody fished – women, men, old people and children.

Rivers, streams and lakes

People who spent a lot of time near rivers streams and lakes caught snails and small reptiles with their bare hands. They soon invented ways of catching the fish in the water. They used stones or clubs to beat large fish such as pike that swim up near the water's surface. Hunting spears were used to catch salmon as they leapt out of the streams and waterfalls.

The first fishing lines were made from tough grass tied to a sharp thorn with a scrap of food attached. The sharp points of the thorn stuck into the fish's mouth when it took the bait. Later, stronger hooks were made using horn or bone.

Fishing with weapons

The weapons that were successful in the hunt – spears and bows and arrows – were also used for fishing. With a bow and arrow, a fisherman could catch fish in the middle of the river while standing on the riverbank. Bows and arrows were more useful than spears for fishing from a distance, as the fisherman could carry several arrows and would not lose his weapon if he missed at the first shot.

Harpoons were spears designed specially for fishing. They had barbed heads so that they would not slide out of the fish's slippery body. They probably also had a strong line attached to them so that the fisherman could pull them back when he had made a catch. The Inuit hunters of North America used to tie animal bladders filled with air to their harpoons so that that if they missed the target the harpoons floated on the water and could be picked up again.

Boats and nets

Fish from the sea became a main source of food as soon as people learned to make boats big and safe enough to sail further than a few hundred metres from the coast.

The earliest boats were dug-out canoes made from hollowed out tree trunks or coracles made from reeds or rushes. They were not easy to control and floated wherever the currents and winds pushed them. When oars were invented, around 8000 BC, people began to build bigger boats and to sail further from land in them.

At first, people caught fish from boats with their hunting weapons. This did not produce a very large or reliable catch. Then people began to make fishing nets using plaited leather thongs, twisted grass fibre or thick animal hair. Scooping a net-load of fish out of the water was quicker than catching them one at a time and provided enough to feed a whole village.

The development of oars and bigger boats changed the way people fished. One or two people did the fishing while a crew of oarsmen rowed the boat. People could row out to sea or across broad rivers to look for new fishing grounds. Until they invented nets, most fishing was done with spears, harpoons or bows and arrows.

DOMESTICATING ANIMALS

The first animals to become part of everyday human life were goats, sheep and cattle. Goats helped to clear land for crop-growing by eating tough, scrubby plants. The flocks would be brought into the settlement at night to save them from being eaten by wolves or lions.

Goats, sheep and pigs

After 12000 BC, when people began to settle down and grow crops, their fields of grain and cereal attracted wild goats, sheep and cattle. These animals ate or destroyed the crops. The settlers could either spend a lot of time defending their fields or tame the animals. Taming the animals saved the crops and provided a source of meat. Goats and sheep were domesticated first. Cows, pigs and chickens followed. Pigs did not eat grass but thrived on meat scraps, cereals, nuts and acorns.

The settlers became herders as well. A single sheep can eat 50 kg of grass in a week, so the flocks had to be moved around the land to find enough to eat. To help them, early shepherds had dogs, which had been domesticated around 11000 BC.

Drying meat

With so much meat available, people had to find ways of preserving it. Drying in the open air was one of the early methods.

Animal products

Domesticated animals provided more than meat. Sheep produced wool and a thick grease called lanolin. Goat skins could be used to make water-tight containers. Pigs gave lard and bristles which were used to make brushes. Cattle, sheep and goats gave milk, which was used to make butter and cheese.

THE FIRST FARMERS

Even when people began to grow crops, they still went hunting for meat. Some people did not settle to the farming life but kept to the old life of hunting and gathering. The hunting tribes often attacked the farmers' settlements to steal food.

A change of climate

Almost 12,000 years ago the climate began to change. It became warmer and drier. Grassy cereal plants such as wild wheat and wild barley began to grow in the improved weather conditions. At first they grew in separate clumps but as each plant produced seeds at the end of summer, more plants grew and soon the clumps spread until there were whole fields covered in wild wheat and barley.

People were used to gathering wild plants growing on the hunting trails. They already knew that seeds from the grassy plants could be crushed up to make a nourishing porridge. The grain began to grow in large quantities all in one place and changed the way people led their lives.

The beginning of farming

At first, people made regular camps by the grain fields in the summer when the grain was ripe, It took at least three weeks to harvest the wild crop, using flint sickles. Gradually, over thousands of years, the summer camps became fixed settlements as people learned how to make the wheat and barley grow better and how to work together to gather a good harvest. They began to store the grain they harvested for use in the winter. There was no longer any need to go out looking for plant food. People could grow it for themselves.

Although they still had to hunt and fish as well, people began to take control of the land. They became farmers.

FARMING IN ANCIENT EGYPT

The fertile Nile

Farming in Ancient Egypt was helped by the River Nile. Every summer, after heavy rain, it flooded its banks. When the water drained away, it left rich, black, fertile soil which was easy to plough. Crops grew easily and an Egyptian farmer could produce three times the amount of food needed to feed his own family. With so much food available, the population quickly increased. A whole new civilization developed, as people were able to develop other skills rather than spending all their time farming or hunting for food.

Irrigating the fields

Egyptian farmers did not rely entirely on the natural flooding of the Nile. To keep their crops watered through the long, hot growing season, they dug a system of canals and ditches. The flood water could be stored in the ditches until it was needed.

To move the water from the ditches the farmers used a *shaduf*, a balanced beam with a bucket at one end and a heavy stone at the other. The weight of the stone pulled the full bucket out of the water so it could be swung round to reach the crops.

Egyptian food crops

Barley and wheat were the earliest crops grown by ancient Egyptians. Their names are written in hieroglyphics, the most ancient known form of writing. Both grains were used to make bread and cakes – there were at least 40 different kinds, some of them made with honey, eggs or milk. Barley was used to make ale.

The Egyptians also grew fruit and vegetables such as onions, garlic, radishes, salad greens, beans, lentils, dates, figs, grapes, apples and olives.

Animals for food and work

Egyptian farmers kept goats, sheep and cattle for meat and milk. Pork was very popular and pigs were kept in special 'kennels'. Ducks and geese were fattened for the table. Wild water birds, eel, carp, perch, mullet and other fish came from the Nile marshes. Some of the fish were dried and salted. People hunted wild animals such as hippos, giraffes and hyenas for food. Dogs were used to guard the herds, donkeys and oxen pulled carts and ploughs and cats pounced on the mice in the grain stores.

Harvesting the crops

There were three seasons in the Egyprtian farmer's year: the flood, the sowing and growing season and harvest time. The Ancient Egyptians developed special tools to help them grow and gather their crops.

As soon as the flood water had gone down, the farmer hoed his land to clear away weeds and stones, then sowed his seeds. The ox trod the seeds into rich soil while the plough behind it turned the soil over to cover the seeds. The crops were harvested in March or April. Farmers cut down the stalks with sickles. The stalks were threshed, or beaten, with a hinged stick called a flail (**1**). This separated the grain from the stalk. Then the grain was heaped up and tossed into the air (**2**). The wind blew away the chaff (husks and bits of stalk) and the heavy grain fell back to the ground. Finally the grain was packed into baskets (**3**) and carried away to grain stores.

FEEDING IMPERIAL ROME

Food from near and far

By the time of the Roman Empire, farming had become well organised. As the Romans conquered more countries, they found new and different kinds of food. Trade with Arab countries brought exotic food and spices.

The Roman farm

Many rich Roman citizens owned large farms or estates outside the city. They grew food to feed themselves and to sell in the market. The farm included meadows, crop fields, kitchen gardens orchards, vineyards, olive groves and cattle pens.

Roman plenty

Wheat, olives and wine grapes were the main crops. Vegetables from the kitchen gardens included peas, beans, leeks, onions, garlic, cabbage, beetroot, marrows, and turnips. The Romans used honey for sweetening food. They kept their beehives next to their orchards so that the bees would take pollen from tree to tree to ensure that fruit would grow. Roman farmers grew apples, pears, figs and grapes.

Milk, cheese and meat came from sheep, goats and cattle. Chickens were popular – and were also used to sacrifice to the gods. Pigeons, snails and dormice were specially fattened up for rich Romans and fish were kept alive and fresh in special ponds called *piscinae*. Exotic foods were brought in from imperial outposts – oysters from Britain, peacocks from Africa. Spices such as pepper and cinnamon came from Arab traders.

groma

corobate

Marking out the fields

A Roman farm was planned out as precisely as a Roman military campaign. To do this accurately, Roman officials used two instruments. The *groma* helped them draw right angles and the *corobate* to measure height.

INSIDE A ROMAN FARM

Roman farmers processed much of the raw material grown on the farm on the spot. They pressed olives to make oil, fermented grapes to make wine, made cheese from goat's milk and ground grain to make flour.

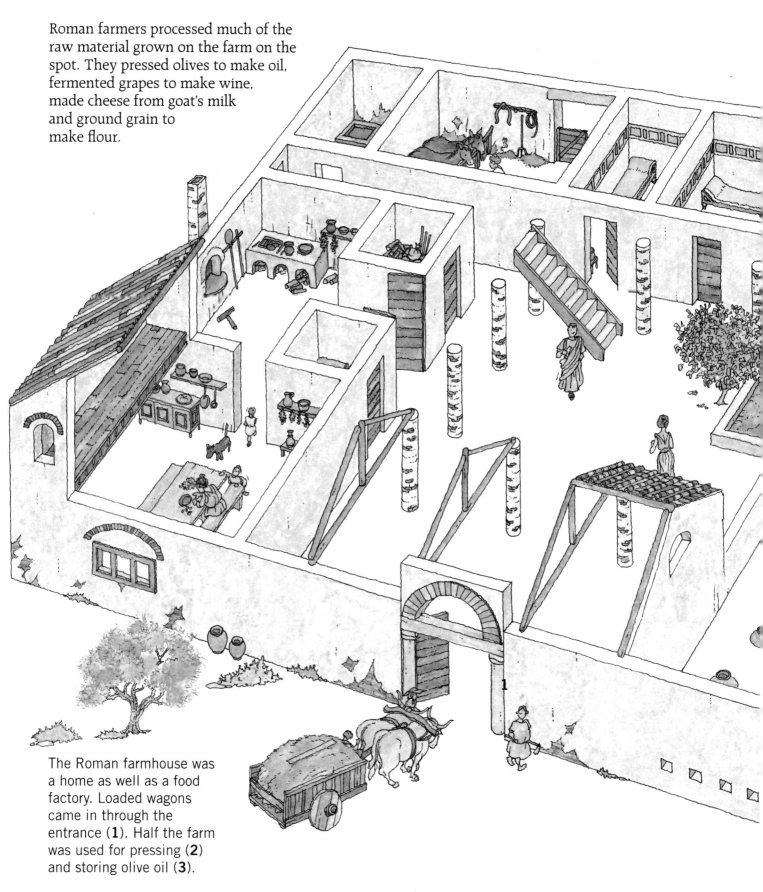

The Roman farmhouse was a home as well as a food factory. Loaded wagons came in through the entrance (**1**). Half the farm was used for pressing (**2**) and storing olive oil (**3**).

Olives and olive oil

Like the Greeks and other Mediterranean peoples, the Romans grew olives for eating and for oil which they used to cook with and to 'butter' their bread. The olives grown for eating were preserved in salt water. Different kinds of olives were used to make oil. They were pressed to release the oil from their flesh. The oil was stored in earthenware pots called *amphorae*.

Grapes and wine

Grape wine was made and drunk in all the countries of the Mediterranean but Roman vineyards could produce over 1600 gallons of wine to the acre and Roman wine became famous. The Romans took vines and wine making all over Europe.

Juice pressed from the grapes was kept in wooden barrels until the sugar in it had fermented into alcohol. Sometimes herbs and spices were added to stop the wine going bad. Then it was stored in *amphorae* or bottles.

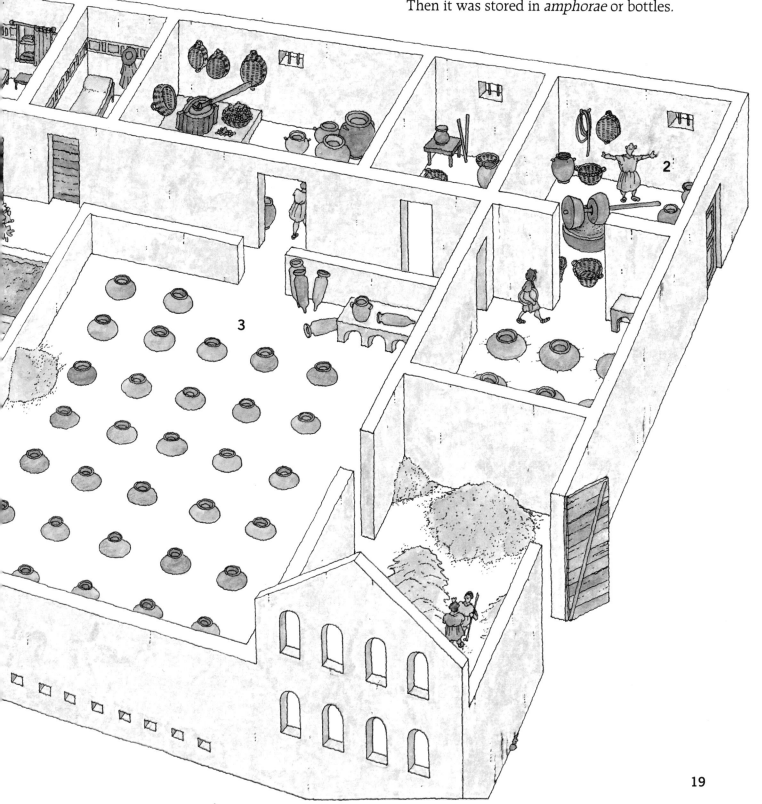

This is the bakery and shop of a Roman miller-baker. He carried out the whole process of breadmaking, from grinding the grain to selling the loaves.

Roman bakers made many different kinds of bread, some plain, some sweet and some savoury. Cheese, milk, honey, aniseed, salt, pepper and oil were all used as flavourings.

ovens

rotary quern

In the rotary quern grain poured in at the top was ground up by the millstone grating against a spindle. Flour flowed out through grooves at the bottom.

BREAD

Paste and porridge

People could not make bread before they had mills or ovens. They ground grains, using a round stone on a flat one, then mixed them with water and to make a grain paste or thick porridge. The Italian *polenta*, made from millet, is a grain paste eaten today.

Flat breads

The earliest sort of bread was flat bread. This was made by burning or heating grains to split them open then grinding them into flour and adding enough water to make a stiff dough. The dough was spread flat and cooked on a hot stone by the fire. People in many countries still make flat bread.

Raised bread

Bread made with yeast so that it rises was probably first baked in Egypt. The Egyptians developed a kind of wheat that did not need to be toasted before the grains could be ground. Historians think that Egyptian bakers experimented by mixing the flour with beer instead of water. Beer contains yeast which gives off gas (carbon dioxide) when it gets warm. When the bread was baked, the bubbles of gas in the dough made it rise.

Milling techniques

People first milled by crushing the grain between a rolling-pin shaped stone and a flat one. Later rotary mills were invented. The grain was ground between two round flat stones grating against each other. The first mills were small and worked by hand. Later, larger versions were pushed round by animals. These produced lots of flour quickly so more bread could be made.

mixing the dough

The Pompeii loaf

When the city of Pompeii was excavated, one of the things found perfectly preserved by volcanic ash was this loaf of bread. It is just the same as the bread made in Italy today.

THE GRAIN TRADE

Wheat for sale

Wheat is a staple food in many countries. Countries that grow more than they need themselves use it to trade with other countries. Wheat stores well and does not rot quickly. The grain trade has gone on for centuries. Middle Eastern traders sold wheat to India and China 4500 years ago. Today, Canada, America and Australia grow wheat to sell to Europe.

The Roman grain trade

Rome had to import large quantities of grain to feed its citizens. All the imported grain went directly to Rome. The rest of the country lived on what it could grow. Some of the grain came from Egypt, the rest from Sicily and North Africa. The constant search for grain was one of the reasons for the expansion of the Roman empire.

Grain was carried in the hold of the ship. Each ship could carry a million kilograms of grain. They could sail from North Africa to Ostia in less than a week and from Egypt in two weeks. In exchange for the grain, the Romans traded their own exports, including wine, oil and pottery.

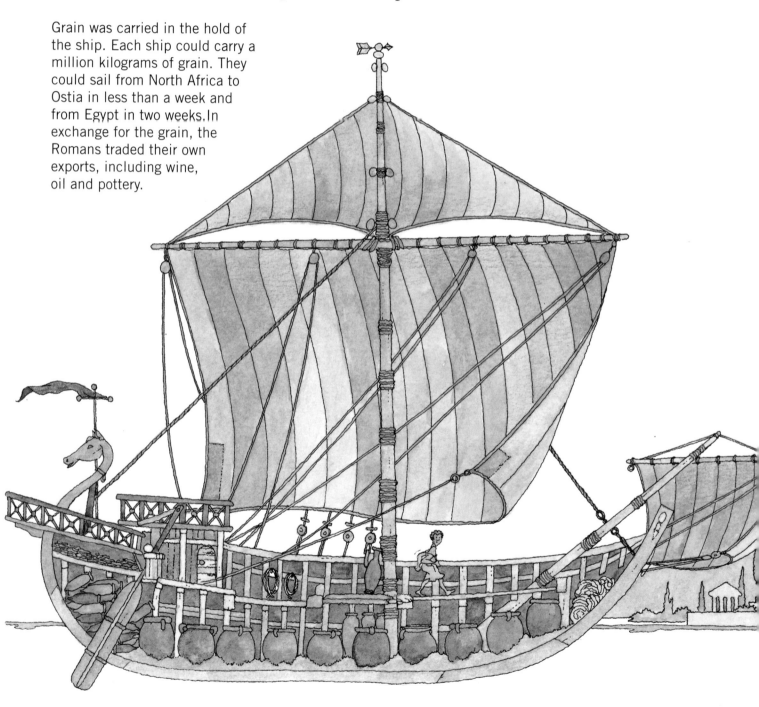

Bread and circuses

Rome needed so much grain because it was given away free to poor citizens. Around AD 100, 320,000 adult males received a free daily ration. Although this helped poor people, it also prevented them making trouble. Roman officials thought that if people had enough to eat and were entertained by circuses and games, they would not question authority.

Shipping the grain

Grain was transported by ship. This was quicker than pulling it in carts overland and large quantities of grain could be moved in one shipment. The ships came in to Ostia, the nearest port to Rome, where special grain docks were built to receive it.

The safe and speedy arrival of the grain was so important that it was against the law for the ships to stop anywhere else on their journey. Captains who landed their ships elsewhere could be put to death.

A sample bag of grain was sealed up and sent separately to be compared with the main shipment. This was to guard against dishonest merchants secretly replacing the cargo with low-quality grain.

When the ship docked at Ostia, the grain was unloaded, checked and stored in guarded warehouses. From there it was packed into barges and sailed up the river to Rome. The journey took three days.

MARKETS, SHOPS AND STREETSELLERS

Market values

As soon as people began to live in towns and cities, they set up markets. The first markets were just stalls collected together but later they had their own special buildings

The market was at the heart of life in the town or city. Many people had no land where they could grow or raise their own food, or only had enough space to grow a few vegetables or keep a chicken or two. They could get what else they needed at the market. Until the invention of refrigeration, canning and other methods of preservation, people had to buy food fresh every day and so went to the market daily. At first, people bartered for food, exchanging goods or other kinds of food for it. Later, when money was introduced, shopping became easier and the shopkeepers became wealthy.

The Greek Agora

In Athens, the market place was called the agora. As Greece is a hot country, the Athenians built a covered market to shield the food on the stalls from the hot sun. This was simply a roof supported on pillars. It was open on all sides. The agora attracted so many stallholders and customers that the Athenians had to introduce market police to prevent cheating and stealing. Selling short weight and disguising food that had gone rotten were common tricks.

Shops and street sellers

People also bought their food from shops. To begin with, these were just the shopkeeper's houses opened up to the customers. The family lived above the shop or at the back.

People who did not have shops sold food in the street. They were called pedlars. Shopkeepers and market stall holders did not like them because they sold their goods very cheaply. However, as they moved on all the time and did not have regular supplies, customers found them unreliable. Many of them also cheated. For example, they picked wild juniper berries, dried them and sold them as expensive peppercorns.

Fast food

Selling ready-to-eat cooked food is not a new idea. Many people did not have ovens to roast meat or bake bread in, so they bought them ready made. There were cookshops in the Near East in Biblical times, in Ancient Egypt, Greece and Rome. In medieval times, cookshops in Europe sold all kinds of meat, fish and poultry, roast, boiled or fried as required. People also took their own meat to the shop to be cooked, just as they took their own dough to be baked at the bakers.

A Roman market

A large city like Rome, with a population of thousands, could support a permanent market site. It was covered to protect the customers and stall holders. It sold everyday food such as figs, olives, beans, honey, parsley, goat's cheese and olive oil, and luxury spices (pepper, ginger, cinnamon and cumin) for the rich. People could also buy *liquamen* in the market. This was a cooking sauce made from pounded anchovies and salt left to ferment in the sun for a few months.

SMALLHOLDINGS AND MONASTIC FARMS

The Dark Ages

Between the 5th and 11th centuries (400-1100) life was very difficult in Europe. The Roman Empire, had come to an end. Fierce tribes led by warrior kings came from Asia and the east of Europe to take land and conquer cities. The well-organized roads and trade routes of the Roman Empire were abandoned. People began to leave the towns and cities. They were afraid of being invaded and they could no longer rely on traders to bring deliver food. They moved to the country.

Most people in Europe at this time lived in small settlements or villages. They became self supporting, growing their own food and bartering with others. They grew small patches of wheat, rye and vegetables; and kept animals

Rye bread and maslin

Most people in Europe ate dark brown bread made from rye flour. Rye began as a weed in the wheatfield. When people discovered that it tasted as good, they began to grow it as a main crop. Wheat was used to make a porridge called frumenty or mixed together with rye to make maslin. Rich people used maslin flour to make light bread and pastry.

Monasteries

At this time, monasteries were set up all over Europe. The monks who lived in them had dedicated their lives to God and learning. They were important centres for the small villages surrounding them, offering protection to the poor and sick. In return, the villages supplied them with food. The monks also grew food for themselves.

People grew enough food for themselves and their family. Most families had a few goats and sheep, so they had milk to drink and make cheese and wool to make clothes. In the small fields around their houses they grew vegetables. Pigs were cheap to keep as they ate acorns and nuts from the forest and they also provided salt pork.

Most monasteries were built around a large church called an abbey (**1**). The monks grew much of the food they needed in vegetable gardens (**2**, **3**, **4**,). One garden (**5**) was for special herbs which the monks used to make medicine. They grew fruit in orchards (**6**) where they also kept bees. The well (**7**) gave them fresh water. Pigs, geese and chickens were kept within the monastery walls, and sheep and goats were herded outside. Fish were kept in a special pool called a *vivarium*.

THE MILL AND THE PLOUGH

New farming techniques

In the Middle Ages in Europe, famine and food shortage were constant threats. It was very important for farmers to sow as many crops as possible and to make sure that every harvest was a success.

To do this, farmers developed new farming techniques. They invented a plough strong enough to work heavy soil and uncultivated land so that they could make new fields. They found quicker ways to drive the mills to grind grain into flour. And they learned not to exhaust the soil by growing the same crop on it year after year.

The three field system

Greek and Roman farmers knew that growing the same crop in the same field makes the soil poor and the crops eventually fail. Each year they left half the field lying fallow so that it could recover. They also knew that legume plants (beans and peas) put goodness back into the soil. The medieval farmers used this information to create the three field system. They planted one field with grain crop, the second with peas, beans or lentils and left the third fallow. The next year the fallow field was used for grain, the grain field for beans and the bean field left fallow, and so on.

The medieval plough

The medieval plough was fixed on a framework between two wheels. The wheels moved the plough more easily over the ground. This design allowed the ploughman to push down hard on the plough as it was drawn along. The metal-tipped plough share, or blade, cut deep into the earth. Deep tilling of the soil made it more fertile. Most ploughs were pulled by oxen, which were slow but very strong. Horses were faster but their feet needed protection from damp soil. When metal horse shoes were invented, most farmers in Europe changed from oxen to horses. A new collar was developed which made it much easier for the animal to pull the plough.

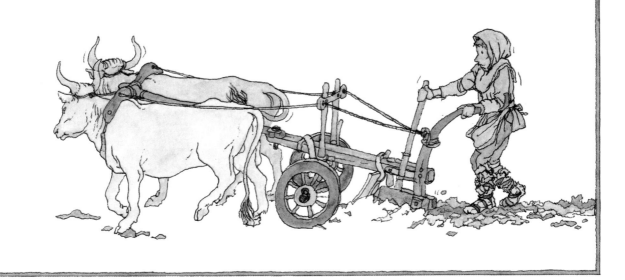

◀ A watermill was like a rotary mill tipped on to its side. The rush of water in the millstream turned a huge wooden wheel outside the mill building attached by a spindle to a second wheel inside. As this wheel turned it drove the millstones round.

Water power

Watermills were developed around the 6th century (500–600). They were powered by the flow of water in a river or stream. Watermills worked all the time using a free source of energy which did not run out, need feeding, or die. They were powerful enough to drive large millstones. Large quantities of grain were ground quickly and economically.

Horse power

The plough had been known from Roman times, but the medieval farmers made improvements to make it cut deeper furrows and move faster. They added wheels and harnessed horses or oxen to pull the plough.

A plough was very expensive. Few farmers could afford to own one so they joined together to share the cost.

Beekeepers used smoke to drive the bees out of the hives so that they could reach the honeycombs inside. The combs were broken up and the honey packed into pots. The broken honeycombs were soaked in water to make mead.

SPICES, SALT AND HONEY

Preserving for the bad times

Salt, spices and honey have always been important foods, valued for their flavours. Until the last century, they were also used to preserve food. When food was plentiful, some of it was dried, salted or pickled for the winter or for when supplies ran low.

Spices for the rich

For centuries, spices have been used in cooking to add flavour or to disguise the unpleasant taste of old or bad meat or fish. The demand for spices, especially pepper, opened up trade routes all over the world. Most hot spices came from India, Indonesia and China. Because they had to be brought from far away places, spices were very expensive. They became a status symbol for the rich, to show off how much they could afford to spend on feeding themselves.

The importance of salt

Before refrigeration and canning, salting was the main method of preserving food, especially meat and fish. Salt pork and bacon were staple winter foods in Europe. Pigs were slaughtered in the autumn when they were fat from eating all summer. The meat was soaked in brine (salt water) or packed in a barrel of ground up salt and sprinkling of spice. Fish was salted in the same way. Salt was also added to butter and cheese to prevent it going rancid. Most salt was made by boiling sea water.

Honey, the ancient sweetener

Long before sugar came to Europe, honey was used to sweeten bread,cakes and drinks and to preserve fruit. It was a very convenient food – ready to use straight from the honeycomb and cheap to produce as bees do not have to be fed.

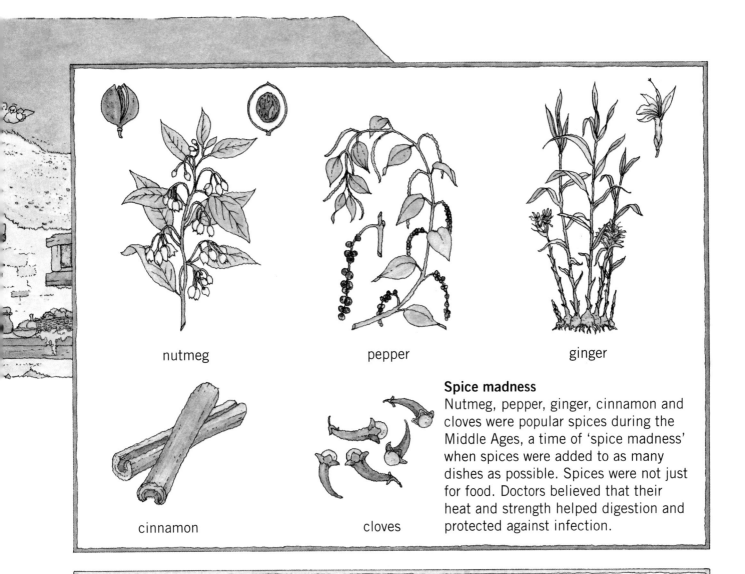

nutmeg

pepper

ginger

cinnamon

cloves

Spice madness

Nutmeg, pepper, ginger, cinnamon and cloves were popular spices during the Middle Ages, a time of 'spice madness' when spices were added to as many dishes as possible. Spices were not just for food. Doctors believed that their heat and strength helped digestion and protected against infection.

Cured meats

Curing means preserving meat so that it can be eaten later. Curing methods include drying, salting, pickling and smoking. The oldest method of drying was to beat the juices out of the meat then leave it in the sun to dry. Later, people cured meat by packing it in a mixture of salt and spice or soaking it in brine to pickle. Often brine-soaked meat was hung over a fire to dry and so became smoked. Below is a selection of cured meats.

ham

salami

sausages

blood pudding

PLAGUE AND PLENTY

The Black Death
In the middle of the 1300s, the terrible plague known as the Black Death swept over Europe. Almost a quarter of the population died. When it was over, there were many changes. There were fewer people to work on the land, more people moved to the towns to live and the population began to rise again. New ways to feed the people were needed. More land was cultivated, new crops tried and new parts of the world explored.

Pastures new
Fertilising and looking after existing fields or leaving them to lie fallow took up too much time when the demand for crops was great. Farmers began to work on land that had not been cultivated before. In the Europe of the 14th century (1300–1400), there was no shortage. Wild areas were ploughed up, forests were cut down and new fields were made, changing the landscape of Europe forever.

New crops

Farmers also looked for new and different crops to grow. In southern Europe, they started to grow maize, the grain brought back from America by Christopher Columbus. Rice had come to Spain in the 7th century (600–700), brought by the Moors who ruled the country at that time. It reached the rest of Europe by the 14th century (1300–1400), but was only grown successfully in Italy.

Expanding horizons

As they could not grow enough for themselves, people began to look for food supplies elsewhere. Trading routes were opened. Huge quantities of grain were imported from eastern Europe through the ports of the Baltic Sea, which were controlled by the Hanseatic League (see below). The grain was so plentiful that some farmers gave up growing their own and began breeding animals for meat instead.

The Hanseatic League

In 1259, the Hanseatic League was founded. Hansa is German for group. The league was a group of towns and ports on or near the Baltic Sea. Lübeck was the centre. The league controlled the trade in grain, herrings, fur and wool. It also opened up overland routes from northern Europe to Venice, the centre of the spice trade. A network of roads and shipping routes now covered Europe and connected it to Africa, India, and the East. All kinds of food stuffs could now be bought and sold all over the known world.

The Herring Trade

The Hanseatic League also controlled the Baltic herring trade. Herrings are oily fish and have to be salted within one day of being caught. Salting sheds complete with barrels and tons of ready ground salt were placed at the dockside so that no time was wasted. North Sea herrings were salted into barrels on board ship.

The salt herring trade flourished in Christian countries, where the Church ordered that people should not eat meat on Fridays or the 40 days of Lent, just before Easter.

FOOD FROM THE NEW WORLD

New tastes for Europe

Columbus and other explorers introduced many new kinds of foods into Europe. Maize and potatoes were quickly accepted, but people at first thought the tomato was just a decorative plant. Cocoa was popular as a drink before it was used to make chocolate.

maize

potatoes

tomatoes

strawberries

sweet pepper

beans

avocado

cocoa bean

peanuts

pineapple

turkey

New food by mistake

When Christopher Columbus set sail in 1492, he was looking for a a new route to the Spice Islands – the East Indies. Instead, he came across the islands of the Caribbean. Other explorers followed him, eventually landing in what is now called South America. During their explorations they came across new kinds of food and took samples back with them.

Columbus first came across maize in Cuba. It was a staple food in many parts of South America including Mexico where the people also grew avocados, green beans, cocoa, sweet peppers, vanilla and tomatoes and raised turkeys. In Peru, the people grew chilli peppers, squashes, peanuts and, high in the Andes where maize could not grow, potatoes.

Sugar and slaves

Europe's discovery of the new world led directly to the slave trade. Sugarcane was introduced into Spain by the Moors. The Spanish found it grew well in the American countries they had conquered. To make production pay, they bought people from Africa to work as slaves on their plantations.

Maize and Potatoes

The new staples

Maize and potatoes arrived in Europe from America in the 16th century. Maize was quickly accepted. The Spanish took it to Italy and Venice. From Venice it went to the Near East and then spread back into northern Europe.

The Spanish also brought potatoes back from Peru. They became popular in Italy as root vegetables and were grated up to make flour, but the French considered them only fit for animal food. Sir Francis Drake brought potatoes back from the Spanish Caribbean colonies and introduced them to England and Ireland, where they became the main crop.

The risks of monoculture

Using land to grow only one crop is called monoculture. Soil used for growing only one crop soon loses its nutrients. Harvests are poor, or fail. If the harvest fails, then there is nothing else to fall back on.

Maize and potatoes were both grown as monoculture crops. The Portuguese took maize to Africa as food for slaves. It lacked essential vitamins and the people suffered from a disease called *pellagra*. The English introduced the potato to Ireland where it became the main crop. In 1845 the harvests failed, thousands died of starvation and many more were forced to emigrate.

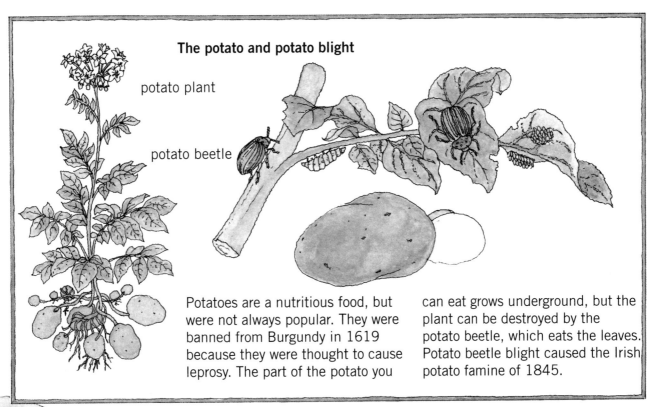

The potato and potato blight

potato plant

potato beetle

Potatoes are a nutritious food, but were not always popular. They were banned from Burgundy in 1619 because they were thought to cause leprosy. The part of the potato you can eat grows underground, but the plant can be destroyed by the potato beetle, which eats the leaves. Potato beetle blight caused the Irish potato famine of 1845.

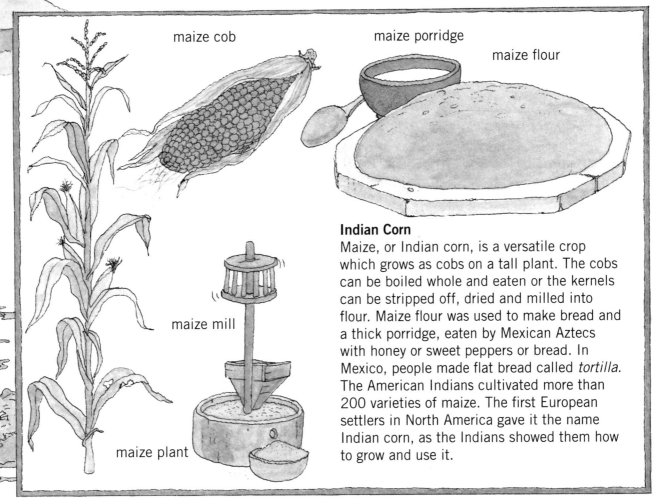

maize cob

maize porridge

maize flour

maize mill

maize plant

Indian Corn

Maize, or Indian corn, is a versatile crop which grows as cobs on a tall plant. The cobs can be boiled whole and eaten or the kernels can be stripped off, dried and milled into flour. Maize flour was used to make bread and a thick porridge, eaten by Mexican Aztecs with honey or sweet peppers or bread. In Mexico, people made flat bread called *tortilla*. The American Indians cultivated more than 200 varieties of maize. The first European settlers in North America gave it the name Indian corn, as the Indians showed them how to grow and use it.

NEW TECHNOLOGY

A new system

From 1700 onwards, the population increased dramatically. Many people stopped working on the land and moved to the new factories created by the industrial revolution. Towns and cities grew rapidly. Constant wars all over Europe led to shortages of food and farm labour. Growing enough food for everybody was once more a problem.

People looked for more efficient ways to keep the soil fertile, grow more crops and process what they harvested. They stopped chopping down forests, introduced a new systems of crop rotation and invented machinery to help them.

New tools and techniques

New tools and machinery turned farming into an industry. Mass produced farm tools were made cheaply from cast iron, introduced in the 1700s. The English landowner Jethro Tull (1674–1741) invented a horse drawn hoe and a mechanical seed drill to plant crops.

New crop rotation systems avoided the need for one field to lie fallow. Most countries used the four crop method, growing wheat, barley, clover and turnips. The clover revived the soil and provided grazing for cattle. Turnips choked weeds and were a good source of winter fodder for animals. Manure produced by the animals fertilised the soil.

Jethro Tull's Seed Drill
The traditional method of sowing crops by scattering was slow and wasted seed.

Tull's invention drilled a seed holes in a straight line and dropped seeds into them.

Windmill power
It was quicker and easier for the farmer to take his harvest to the local windmill to be ground. Milling became a separate industry to farming. Shown below is a post mill. The wind drove the sails (**1**) which moved the brakewheel (**2**). This drove the wallower (**3**) which turned the millstones. The miller poured grain into the hopper (**4**) which funnelled it down to the millstones encased in a vat (**5**).The body of the mill could rotate so the sails faced into the wind. The miller pushed it round with a tail pole (**6**).

THE AMERICAN PRAIRIES

The wheatfields of the West

Wheat was introduced into America by European settlers and grew well. Maize was already grown by the American Indians. After the American Civil War (1861-1865), people began to cultivate the huge prairies of the midwest. There was so much land that American farmers did not need to use a crop rotation system, but there were not enough people to grow and harvest the crops. Machines were developed to do the work.

Reapers, threshers and combine harvesters

Cyrus Hall McCormick (1809-1884) was the first person to put machinery to work on the land. He developed a mechanical reaper to harvest the crops. Others invented the mechanical thresher (driven by horses on a treadmill) and the binder and baler, which tied the grain stalks up into sheaves. Last came the combine harvester. This machine cut threshed and cleaned the wheat as it rolled steadily across the prairie. Harvesters were also made to reap maize.

The granary of Europe

The railroad developed at the same time as the new farm machinery. The huge harvests were sent by train to ports on the east coast and then shipped to Europe. The supply of cheap grain discouraged European farmers from growing their own. Some began dairy farming instead, or grew fruit and vegetables. Others turned to livestock. Many farmers emigrated to America where their grain-growing skills were needed.

Although the machinery was steam driven, the machine itself was pulled by horses. By 1900, there were more than 15 million draught horses in America.

The cattle ranges

The prairies and the railroad also made it possible to produce large quantities of beef. Texas ranchers moved their cattle to the prairies to graze. People began to breed cattle especially to produce animals that gave more meat. The cattle went by railroad to cities in the north, such as Chicago, where they were slaughtered. The cost of transportation made the price of beef too high for most people.

collecting sap from sweet maple trees

maple leaf

Maple syrup

Until the late 1800s, people in America and Canada used maple syrup instead of expensive cane sugar to sweeten their food. Maple sap was collected through metal spouts pushed into the tree. Then it was boiled until it turned into syrup. If left boiling for longer, it became sugar.

maple syryp and pancake

Steam Engines on the Farm

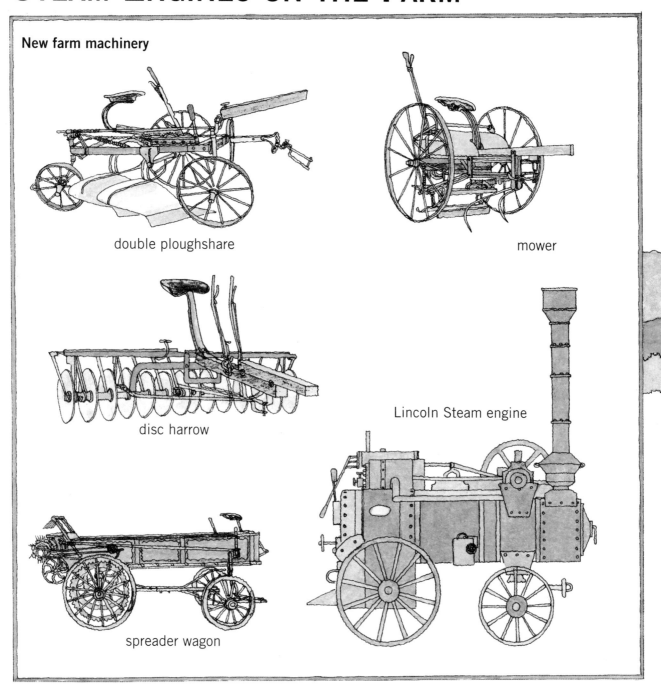

New farm machinery

double ploughshare

mower

disc harrow

Lincoln Steam engine

spreader wagon

The Industrial Revolution
The Industrial Revolution began in England in the 1700s and had spread to the rest of Europe and America by the 1800s. The steam engine, invented in 1698 by Thomas Savery, an English army officer, was improved by the Scottish engineer James Watt (1736–1819). He made it possible for the steam engine to turn the wheels so that it could be used to drive machinery. The first steam engines were used to pump water from mines but they soon found a use on the farm.

Iron and steam
Machines had already been invented to work on the farm using iron, now made cheaply in great quantities. One example was the threshing machine invented by the American brothers John and Hiram Pitts in 1834. It could strip the ears of wheat from the straw and separate the wheat from the chaff to produce clean grain.

Iron was used to make strong plough shares that could cut deeper than wooden ones. Iron was also used to make the disc harrow.

The Industrial Revolution
Powerful steam engines could be used to pull the plough or other farm machinery. The engines did not move themselves. A chain linked the plough with the engine. The engine turned a winch to wind the chain in and tow the plough along. The early farm machines were not very efficient at first, but they quickly improved.

The disc harrow replaced the traditional harrow's teeth with metal discs which could be weighted down so that they would cut deeper.

But all this machinery was powered by horses which either pulled it along or turned treadmills to drive it. One steam engine could do the work of hundreds of horses. Farmers were quick to realise that the new source of power would help them produce more crops. Soon the countryside was shattered with the noise of steam engines.

Crops or people?
When farmers began to use machines on the land, they were able to grow more crops. Because the machines could plough, sow, reap and thresh so much quicker than men, the farmer could cultivate new land to make more fields to sow. On the other hand, the machines put people out of work. People who had worked on the land for generations had to move into towns to look for jobs in the new factories. Many Europeans could not find work and so emigrated to America.

FREEZING AND CHILLING

A cold start

Freezing and chilling food to preserve it is not new. Neolithic hunters left surplus meat in the cold to chill for later use.

At first, people stored ice made naturally in rivers, ponds or mountains. In the 8th century, the Chinese had discovered how to store the ice made made in the winter for use in the summer. They kept it in deep caves or in specially built ice houses, which they kept cool by pouring water over them. Ice houses were also built in the 1700s in England and America.

Ice machines and refrigerators

In the 1830s, the first ice making machines were made. Ice became available all year round. Blocks of it were made in large factories. People bought ice every day to put in wooden ice-boxes where they kept their food cool.

By 1870, a way to chill or freeze food directly was found. This was called refrigeration. Food was frozen in large quantities in factories. A few years later, refrigeration units were built into ships so that frozen food could be kept cold on long journeys. In the 1920s, an American called Clarence Birdseye invented deep freezing, a way to cool food quickly so that it froze solid and kept for longer.

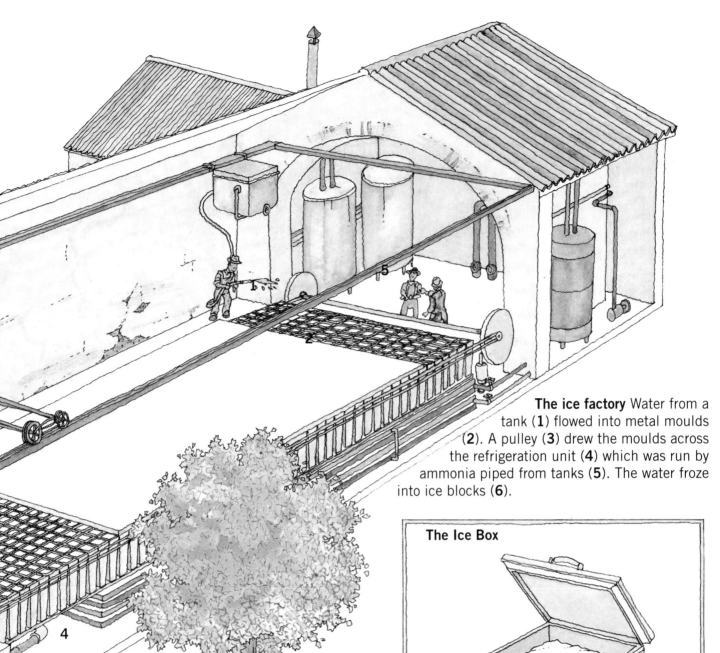

The ice factory Water from a tank (**1**) flowed into metal moulds (**2**). A pulley (**3**) drew the moulds across the refrigeration unit (**4**) which was run by ammonia piped from tanks (**5**). The water froze into ice blocks (**6**).

Bananas and ice cream

Once food was frozen or chilled, it could be safely sent all over the world. In 1877, the SS *Paraguay* carried the first cargo of frozen beef from Argentina to France. Meat was sent to Europe from America, Australia and New Zealand. Fruit and vegetables could also be chilled for export. Bananas from the West Indies were eaten in Europe for the first time in the late 1800s.

Ice cream was probably first made in Italy around 1550. With refrigeration, it could be factory-made in large quantities and became a favourite food in Europe and America.

The Ice Box

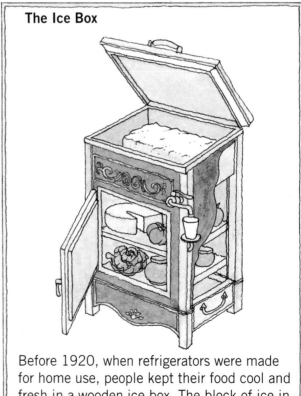

Before 1920, when refrigerators were made for home use, people kept their food cool and fresh in a wooden ice box. The block of ice in the top compartment was replaced every day.

CANNING FOOD

Glass jars and tin cans

In the 1800s most people lived in towns and worked in factories and could not grow their own food. Farmers and animal breeders raised more than enough food to supply everybody. The problem was how to presrve it.

Canning was one answer. In 1809, a French sweet maker, Nicolas Appert, experimented with ways to preserve food for Napoleon's army. Appert thought that air spoiled food and that sealing food away from air would stop it going bad. He packed food into glass jars, sealed them with corks than plunged them into boiling water. The heat killed the germs in the food.

In England, Appert's method was used but the food was packed into tin cans which were light and unbreakable. A canning factory was opened in 1812. William Underwood took the idea to America and opened the first canning factory there in 1820 in Boston.

Convenience food

The first tin cans were hand made. After 1868, they were mass produced by machine. The canning factories introduced assembly lines to can the food more quickly and cheaply. At the same time, farmers using harvesting machines produced large quantities of food to be canned.

All kinds of food was canned. It had to be cooked first or packed into the can in a liquid, otherwise the can would explode when it was boiled. Vegetables were packed in salt water, fruit in sugar syrup, fish in oil or brine. Meat was pickled in brine, boiled or stewed.

The first customers for canned food were soldiers, sailors, travellers and explorers. It was fairly light to carry and kept for years. When mass production started, canned food became cheap enough for ordinary people to buy. It was popular because it kept for a long time and gave people a chance to taste different food and vary their daily diet.

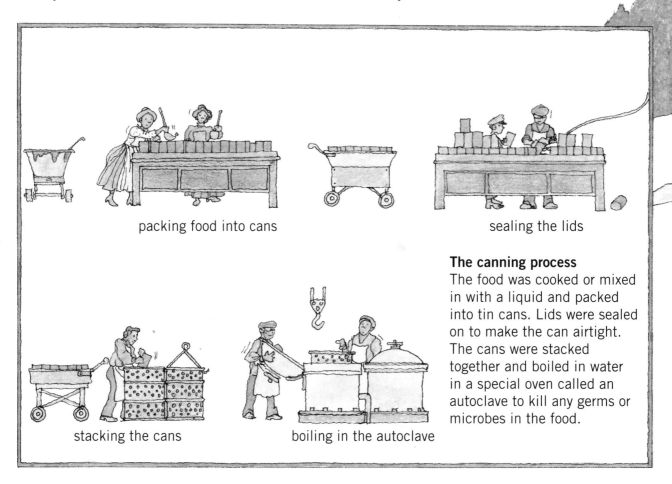

packing food into cans

sealing the lids

stacking the cans

boiling in the autoclave

The canning process
The food was cooked or mixed in with a liquid and packed into tin cans. Lids were sealed on to make the can airtight. The cans were stacked together and boiled in water in a special oven called an autoclave to kill any germs or microbes in the food.

The can opener
The first can opener was invented in 1858. It was not very efficient. The first winding can opener was made in 1925.

winding can opener

INTENSIVE FARMING

Overworking the land

In small countries or countries where not much land is available or suitable to grow crops, the farmers have to find ways to grow as much as possible in a small space. In Japan, for example, the farmers build terraces to grow their rice. This is called intensive farming.

Another kind of intensive farming is to grow only one or two kinds of crop and to get as many harvests as possible from the same area of land.

Fertilisers and the food chain

Intensive farming does not let the land rest so it needs fertilisers to give back the nutrients that the crops take out and pesticides to keep kill insects and weeds. Scientists have developed very powerful chemicals to do these jobs.

Although these chemicals help farmers to grow more crops, they also cause problems. Rain washes the chemicals into the water supply, where they become part of the food chain. They affect plants, animals and humans.

Terrace farming

To get the best use of mountainous land, farmers in some countries make terraces. This provides as much flat land as possible in a small space and drains off rainwater. Inca farmers made terrace fields for maize.

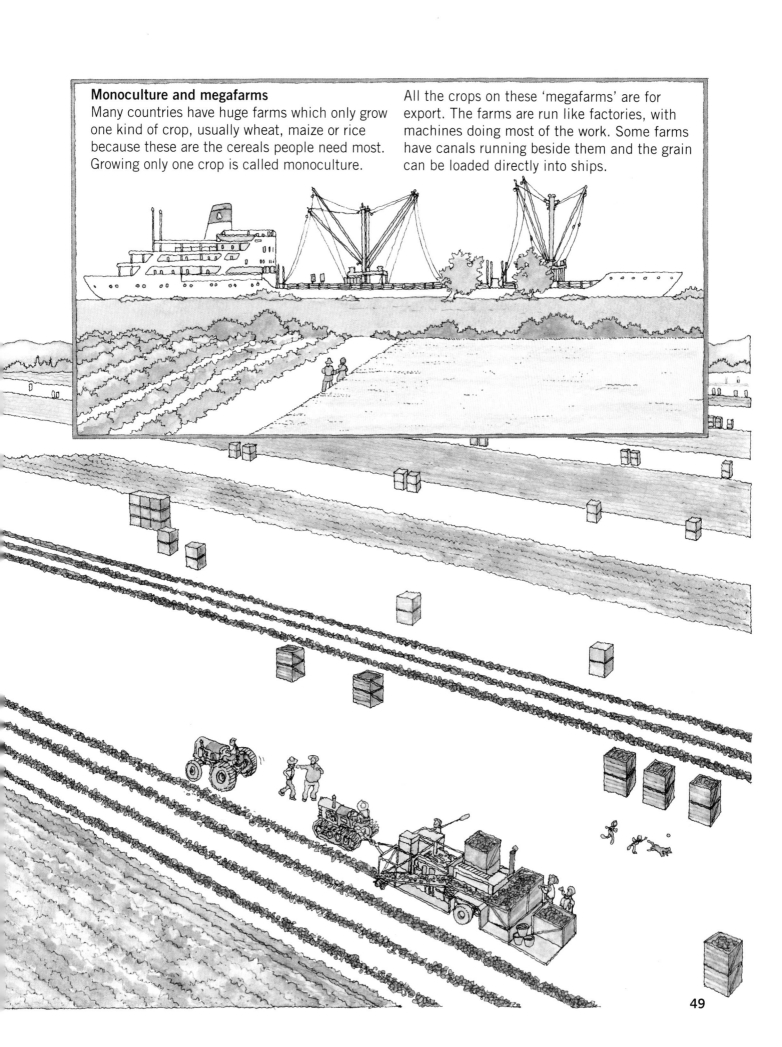

Monoculture and megafarms

Many countries have huge farms which only grow one kind of crop, usually wheat, maize or rice because these are the cereals people need most. Growing only one crop is called monoculture.

All the crops on these 'megafarms' are for export. The farms are run like factories, with machines doing most of the work. Some farms have canals running beside them and the grain can be loaded directly into ships.

BREEDING ANIMALS

Pig breeds

Wild boar

Pigs were domesticated about 8000 BC. They were bred from wild boars. Modern pigs are bred to produce meat (pork), bacon or fat, or because they produce large litters of piglets.

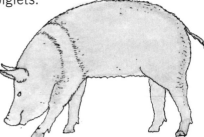
The Hampshire produces lean meat

The Duroc produces large litters of piglets

The Yorkshire produces large amounts of bacon

Early breeding

People have herded cattle and sheep since prehistoric times. When they began to breed them by selection, they killed off the weaker ones or those that did not produce enough. They did not try to breed the animals for only one thing; they kept sheep for milk, meat and wool; they kept cattle for milk, meat and pulling loads.

Early selective breeding was almost accidental. In the Middle Ages, most people had only a few animals – some sheep, a pig or two, one cow. As animals were expensive to feed over the winter, they would kill the weaker ones in the late autumn, keeping the strongest for breeding the next year. Strong animals breed more strong animals and so the stock was improved.

Meat or milk?

Modern cattle breeding methods began in the 1700s when an English farmer called Robert Bakewell looked for ways to improve his cattle so that they would produce more meat. Since then farmers have bred cattle either for their milk or for their beef, although some can be used for both. Some dairy cattle are used for meat. Young dairy bulls, who cannot produce milk, are killed for veal.

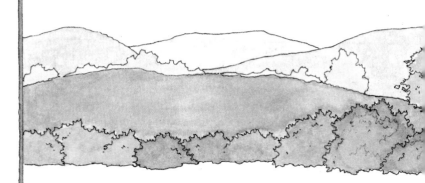

Fixed stabling

These beef cattle are shut in a stall and only eat prepared feed from a trough. This system of cattle raising is called fixed stabling.

This method gives more meat because the animal is prevented from moving around too much and doesn't grow muscular and tough.

Beef mountain

Breeding cattle for meat really took off in America in the late 1800s. The North American Indians and the buffalo they depended on had been driven off the endless prairies. Texan ranchers put their huge herds of cattle to graze there instead.

Columbus had taken some Spanish cattle to the West Indies in 1493 where they bred well. Some of their descendants were taken to Mexico and later to Texas. The Texas Longhorn cattle were bred from them. Cattle were imported from Europe to improve the native Longhorn breed. The Hereford was introduced from England in 1817 and the Aberdeen Angus from Scotland in 1873. The cross breeding produced cows that gave very good quality meat and bred quickly. By 1900 there were almost 60 million cattle in the USA.

Beef cattle do not graze the grasslands as dairy cattle do. They do not need the grass to make milk. When they are a few months old they are kept in pens and fed concentrated feedcakes to fatten them up quickly for market.

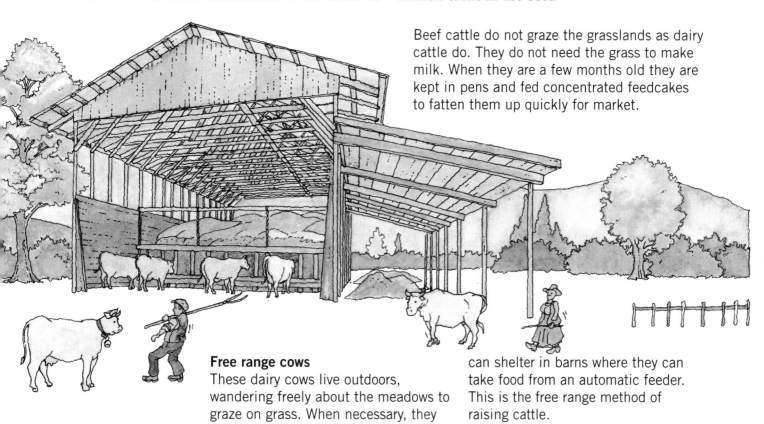

Free range cows

These dairy cows live outdoors, wandering freely about the meadows to graze on grass. When necessary, they can shelter in barns where they can take food from an automatic feeder. This is the free range method of raising cattle.

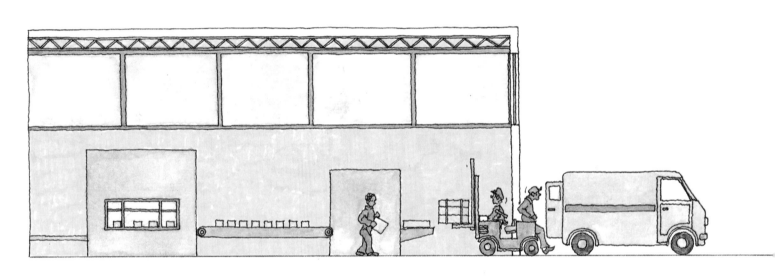

Louis Pasteur
Louis Pasteur (1822-1895) was a French scientist who discovered that food goes rotten because bacteria breed in it. He invented a way to stop the bacteria spreading in milk. The milk is heated to 63°C for at least 30 minutes then chilled quickly to below 10°C. and kept cool. This process is called pasteurization.

From the cow to the customer

The milk from the cow goes straight from the milking machine through cooling tanks to the milk tanker which is insulated to keep the milk cool. The tanker takes it to the creamery where it is pasteurized and packed in bottles or cartons.

THE DAIRY INDUSTRY

Early days

When sheep, cattle and goats were domesticated, milk became an important part of people's diet. At first, they probably simply drank it, but soon they noticed that it had other uses. Milk left to stand separates into cream and skimmed milk. If the cream is kept longer it turns into soft cheese. The first butter may have been churned by accident when someone took a goat's skin bag of milk on a long bumpy ride. People discovered that cheese and butter, mixed with a little salt, did not spoil as quickly as milk. They began to make butter and cheese as a way of storing milk.

In medieval Europe, when there were more sheep than people, most butter and cheese was made from ewe's milk. Most people made their own butter and cheese at home.

From farm to factory

As late as the 1850s raw milk straight from the cow was sold in towns and cities. As towns grew larger and fields were built over, there was nowhere for the cows to graze. Milk had to be brought in from the country. People began to look for ways to keep milk fresh. Canned condensed milk was introduced in 1856 but the most important developments came in the 1860s and 1870s with pasteurization and refrigeration. Pateurization killed the bacteria in milk and chilling kept it fresh.

Butter and cheese used to be made on the farm. As demand grew, farmers concentrated on milk production. They used milking machines, invented in 1918, and sent their milk to factories called creameries to be churned into butter, cream and cheese.

A Balanced Diet

Until the last century, most people's jobs involved hard physical work, most people walked or rode on horseback to where they wanted to go and houses were not well heated. People did not worry about getting fat but about getting enough food to keep them warm, to keep their body systems working and to give them energy to work.

Now most people in the western world work in offices or in jobs where they sit down all day. They travel to work by car, bus or train. Machines do most of the heavy housework and

Below you can see how many calories an hour everyday activities burn up. A calorie is a unit of energy.

sleeping 65

sitting 100

reading out loud 105

sweeping 168

walking normally 200

walking rapidly 300

Different jobs, different needs

The Office Worker – Daily needs: 2600 calories
Office workers who are sitting down for most of the day do not use up much energy. They should eat 90g of protein, 82g of fat and 387g of carbohydrate a day. Below is a sample daily diet.

The Tailor – Daily needs 3500 calories
Tailors spend a lot of the day standing up and so need more energy than an office worker. They need to eat 105g each of fat and protein and 600g of carbohydrate. A sample daily diet is shown below.

 fish 150g
 eggs 2
 oil 50g
 butter 25g
 sugar 350g

 jam 30g
 vegetables 300g
cheese 40g
fruit 400g

 fish 150g
eggs 2
 oil 25g
 butter 25g
sugar 30g

 jam 40g
 vegetables 200g
 cheese 30g
 fruit 200g
 honey 50g

central heating keeps houses warm. Food is plentiful and easy to get.

Many people now eat more than they need. The energy they do not use up in work and play is stored around their bodies as fat. Some people take up sport and exercise in their spare time to burn up the extra energy. Other people diet by eating fewer fat and sugary foods or by eating special foods that are low in calories.

The diet food industry

A whole industry has grown up to supply special food products for people who want to lose weight. One of the earliest of these was saccharin, the artificial sweetener discovered in 1879. It is 500 times sweeter than sugar but contains no calories at all. Diet food is made by replacing the fat or sugar in ordinary food with low-calorie ingredients.

standing 125

driving 133

typing 144

walking down stairs 365

swimming 430

climbing up stairs 1100

The Manual Worker – Daily needs: 4130 calories
Labourers, bricklayers, carpenters, farmers and other people who work with their hands need lots of energy. They should eat 125g of fat, 634 g of carbohydrate and 118 g of protein. Below is a sample daily diet.

The Removal Man – Daily needs: 4900 calories
Furniture removers, roadmenders and other people who have to move heavy equipment use a great deal of energy. They should eat 153g of fat, 751 g of carbohydrate and 133 g of protein a day. Below is a sample daily diet.

fish 225g	jam 50g
eggs 2	vegetables 400g
oil 40g	chese 30g
butter 20g	fruit 500g
sugar 50g	honey 80g

fish 225g	jam 100g
eggs 2	vegetables 500g
oil 60g	cheese 40g
buuetr 25g	fruit 600g
sugar 100g	honey 80g

Freeze drying

In the freeze drying process the food is first frozen so that the water in it turns to ice. Then it is put in a vaccuum chamber and heated until all the ice evaporates, leaving the food dry. This process does not shrink the food. It is used to preserve coffee, tea and herbs.

Quick freezing

Quick freezing is a way of preserving fresh or pre-cooked food to keep its flavour and juiciness. The food is packed and sealed and then very quickly frozen to a temperature of −40°C. Fish is quick frozen as soon as it is caught to keep it as fresh as possible.

Condensing

Liquid food is condensed by heating it in vaccuum tanks to remove two thirds of its water content. The finished product is sealed in cans which are heated to kill germs. Milk and soup can be preserved this way. Condensed milk has sugar added to help preserve it.

MODERN CONSERVATION METHODS

New ways to preserve food

People now buy more processed and preserved food than they did. Most of us lead busy lives and do not have the time to shop every day for fresh food or the time to prepare it. People now do most of their shopping once a week in super-markets where they can buy many kinds of food specially prepared and packaged so that they will keep fresh for a long time in the refrig-erator or freezer. Because so many foods can be preserved and brought in from all over the world we now have a wider variety of food to choose from than people did 30 years ago.

Some ways of keeping food fresh are not new ideas. Since ancient times, people have dried food, either in the sun or wind. Dried food was not processed on a large scale until

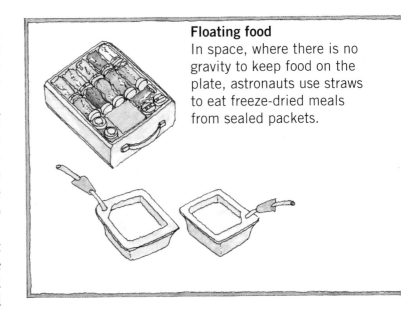

Floating food

In space, where there is no gravity to keep food on the plate, astronauts use straws to eat freeze-dried meals from sealed packets.

Vaccuum packing

Vaccuum packing removes all the air from the can or package so that the food inside will stay fresh for a long time. Coffee, peanuts and many other foods are preserved this way. As soon as the can or package is opened and food is exposed to air, it must be kept cool.

Drying

The oldest method of drying food is sun drying. Modern methods blast hot air over the food to dry it quickly. A slower method is to dry the food on racks in a special oven called a kiln. Fruit and vegetables can be dried but they shrink in the process.

Dehydration

Dehydration is a method of drying liquid food so much that it turns to powder. The liquid is sprayed into special drying chambers. The water in it evaporates and the food particles sink to the bottom of the chamber as powder. Soup, milk and eggs can be dehydrated.

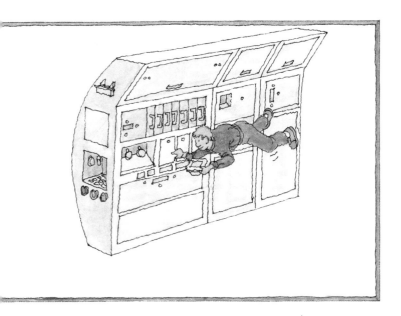

World War II when it was developed for soldiers' rations because it was light to carry. They had dried egg, milk and coffee. Dried or dehydrated food is easy to prepare as it only needs water to be added to it.

Canned food has been available since the 1820s and frozen food since the 1920s. Although more food is canned, frozen food is now an enormous industry. Almost every kind of food is now available frozen.

More recent developments include freeze drying, vaccuum packing and pre-cooked food. Whole dishes are prepared and cooked or partly cooked by the manufacturers and then frozen or chilled. Then the cooking can be finished off in the kitchen at home.

FACTORY FISHING

The fishing industry

Although people had been sea fishing since Neolithic times, it was not until the 20th century that fishing became an industry. When steam turbine engines and diesel engines were developed in the late 1800s it became possible for ships to travel faster and further. Around the same time, refrigeration was invented and fishing boats could put their catch on ice and stay out at sea for longer.

Until the 1960s, the catch was landed at a port where it was processed and frozen at the dockside. Then on-ship freezing plants were introduced. The catch could be processed and deep frozen on the ship which could carry on fishing with its catch safely stored in the hold.

The floating factory

The factory ships are at sea for as long as six months at a time. They are a combined fishing boat, factory, cold store and hotel. The bridge (**1**) is the command centre. Radar and radio signals are picked up in the radar room (**2**). The Captain's cabin (**3**) is near the bridge, as is the crew's day room (**4**) where they can relax when off duty.

From 1900 on the demand for fish grew. Fleets of fishing boats driven by engines rather than steam or sail found new fishing grounds. More efficient nets and machinery for winching them, electronic aids such as radar, sonar and radio satellite helped the fishermen to catch 30 times as many fish as they did in 1900.

The factory ship

Factory ships are much larger versions of the 1960s fishing boats. They catch the fish, process it on board and deep freeze it. Factory ships usually sail with a fleet of fishing boats. Often they process the catch from other boats as well as the fish they catch themselves. The smaller boats pass over the lines attached to their nets and the factory ships use them to winch it on board. This leaves the small boats free to catch more fish.

Factory ships are usually trawlers. They drag a huge bag-shaped net behind them to scoop up huge number of fish. Cod and halibut are caught this way. To catch herring, which swim near the bottom of the sea, the trawl net is weighed down so it drags along on the sea bed to trap large numbers of fish.

Unfortunately the factory ships are are so successful at catching fish that they may soon empty the oceans. The fish left behind cannot breed quickly enough.

The business end

This is a stern trawler. The huge, full net (**5**) is winched on board at the stern, or back of the ship. One end of the net is opened and the fish pour down a chute onto a conveyor belt (**6**) which takes them to the preparation room (**7**). Processed fish is deep frozen and packed away in blocks in the cold store (**8**) which is kept at −20°C.

FOOD IN THE FUTURE

New science

Scientists are looking for new ways to make food grow better. One new technique is genetic engineering which can help to breed stronger plants and animals and to create completely new kinds.

Breeding by selection

Farmers have known about breeding plants by selection for thousands of years. When they first began to cultivate wild wheat and barley, they discovered that they got a better harvest if they thew out diseased or damaged plants and used seeds from the strongest plants to sow for next year's crop.

People also bred animals by selection, killing off the stunted or diseased ones and keeping the strong. They noticed which animals were bigger or stronger or produced more meat, and bred from them.

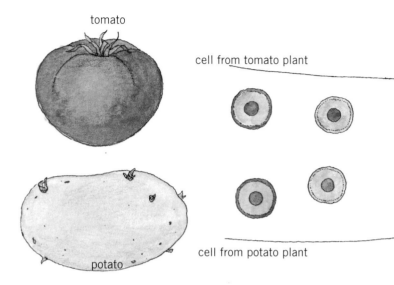

tomato

cell from tomato plant

potato

cell from potato plant

The hybrid plant produces	1000 seeds	after three years and six generations you have a 'pure strain'	350 seeds	**A pure breed** A pure bred animal or a pure strain of plant is produced by selection. Starting with the seeds or young from a hybrid plant or animal, breeders choose those with the characteristics they want and breed them with each other. They repeat this for several generations, depending on the species, until the new pure breed is produced. Pure breeds produce fewer seeds or young than the hybrids but the quality is very high.
The hybrid chicken produces	200 eggs	after nine years and nine generations you have a pure breed which produces	80 eggs	
The hybrid sow has	14 piglets	after 18 years and nine generations you have a pure breed which produces	four piglets	

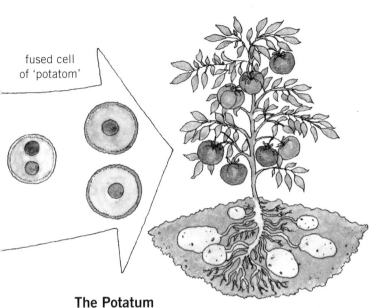

fused cell
of 'potatom'

The Potatum

Plant scientists are working on a cross between a tomato and a potato, which they call a 'potatom'. Cells from the tomato are fused with seeds from the potato to produce a plant which would grow tomatoes on the bushy part above ground and potatoes at the roots underneath.

Breeding a hybrid

Hybrid plants are stronger and produce more fruit or seed than their parent plants. Breeders develop them by crossing different plants with each other. For example, plant **a** and **b** produce a seed **ab**; the plant from this seed is fertilised by a plant **c**, to produce seed **abc**; the plant from seed **abc** is fertilised with plant **d**, to produce the seed **abcd**. This is the hybrid.

Hybrids

Hybrids are produced when slightly different plants (or animals) breed together successfully to form a new species. Hybrid plants and animals are stronger and more productive than their parents and so are good sources of food. To produce a good hybrid, the plants have to be cross bred several times.

Genetic engineering and cellular fusion

Genetic engineering saves time. Instead of breeding generations of animals and plants until they get the characteristics they want, scientists can now work on the plant or animal genes directly and alter them. Cellular fusion allows scientists to take genetic codes from the cells of different plants (or animals), fuse them together and form a new cell and so produce an entirely new plant or animal.

Future food?

Scientists can now make carbohydrates, protein, fats and vitamins in the laboratory, sometimes from the most unlikely sources. Protein, for example, can be made from soy beans or the liquid waste left over when sugar beet is refined. With these basic building blocks any food can be created. Perhaps in the future food will no longer be grown but made in huge laboratory factories.

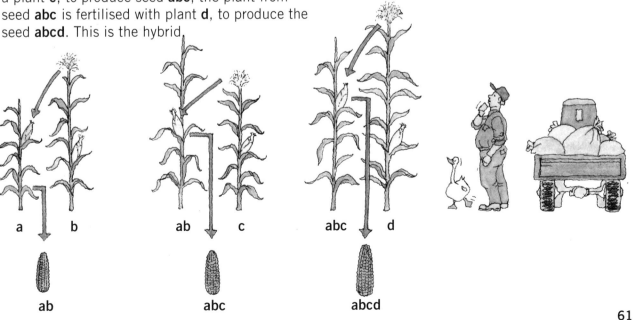

a   b   ab   c   abc   d

ab   abc   abcd

GLOSSARY

amphora Cylinder-shaped earthenware pots used by the Greeks and Romans to store wine, oil, honey or grain. A standard Roman amphora held 25.5 litres.

assembly line A way of processing goods in a factory. A conveyor belt takes the product past a group of workers or machines. At each stage, the workers or machines carry out a different part of the process.

autoclave A special oven used to sterilize cans of food. The cans are heated to a high temperature to kill any germs inside them.

barley Grain plant used to make bread and animal food; dried barley is called malt and is used to make beer and whisky.

barter Exchanging goods for other goods without using money.

blight A plant disease which attacks leaves, stalks and fruit.

brine Very salty water.

calorie A way of measuring energy; one calorie is the amount of energy needed to heat one gram of water by 1°C. The number of calories in an amount of food tells us how much energy that food will produce when it is eaten.

carbohydrate One of the three kinds of food essential to the body; carbohydrates come from sugar and starchy food such as bread, beans and potatoes. See also **fat, protein**.

carcase Dead body of an animal.

cereal General name for grain products.

coracle Small round boat made from woven reeds or grasses.

crop rotation Growing a different crop every year in the same field so that the soil does not become exhausted; crop rotation systems are based on three, four and seven field systems.

cultivate To prepare the land for growing crops.

cure To preserve meat or fish by salting or drying it.

Dark Ages The early centuries of the Middle Ages from about AD 400 to AD 1000.

digestion The process of breaking food down in the body.

export To sell goods and food to another country.

fallow Cultivated land left unplanted for a season so that the soil can rest.

famine Mass starvation that occurs when crops fail because of plant disease, bad weather, floods etc.

fat One of the three kinds of food essential to the body; fat comes from meat, butter, cheese and oil. See also carbohydrate, protein.

fermentation A chemical change in certain foods that change the taste, smell and sometimes the form of the food. For example, the sugar in grapes ferments into alcohol to make wine.

fertile Able to grow and reproduce.

fertiliser Chemical or natural substance fed to plants to make them grow faster or larger.

fodder Food for animals.

food chain The link between the eater and the eaten. Plants are at the bottom end of the food chain; mammals and humans are at the top.

fungi Very simple form of plant life without leaves or green colouring.

genetic engineering Changing the way an animal or plant develops by altering part of the chemical information carried in its genes.

gene Part of the body cell that controls the way a plant or animal grows.

germ Tiny living thing that can reproduce itself to cause disease

graze To eat grass; cattle, sheep and goats graze.

harrow Farming tool used to break up clods of earth thrown up after land has been ploughed.

harpoon A barbed spear with a line attached used to catch fish.

hoe Farming tool used to pull out weeds from between crops and to loosen tightly-packed soil.

hold (ship) Space for cargo in a ship.

hopper A box with a funnel shaped hole at the bottom end.

import To buy and bring in goods or food from other countries.

Indian corn Another name for maize.

kiln Special oven used to dry food; a furnace at the base of the kiln provides the heat and the food is dried on slatted floors above the furnace.

laboratory A place where scientists carry out experiments.

livestock Domesticated animals.

maize Cereal plant used for making corn or as animal food.

mature To become ripe or fully developed.

mead Ale made from honey and water.

meadow Uncultivated grassy land used to graze cattle.

microbe General name for bacteria and viruses that are invisible to the naked eye.

Middle Ages The period in European history from about AD 500 to 1500.

millet Cereal plant grown for grain and animal food.

monasteries Self-contained establishments run by monks and guided by special rules. Many monasteries in the Middle Ages became prosperous farming and sheep-rearing communities.

monoculture Growing only one kind of crop on a large area of land.

Moors Another name for Arab peoples of North Africa. The Moors conquered the southern half of Spain in the 700s.

Neolithic Age The later part of the Stone Age, after

8000 BC, when farming and the domestication of animals began.

oats Cereal crop grown for eating as porridge, making into bread, and to put in animal food.

pellagra Disease caused by lack of vitamin B. People who live mainly on corn and do not eat much meat are likely to suffer from pellagra. It causes skin rashes, digestive troubles and, if untreated, madness.

pesticide Chemical substance made to destroy plant pests.

pickle To pack food in vinegar or salt water (sometimes with spices) to preserve them.

prairies Large area of flat or rolling land covered with various grasses.

protein One of the three kinds of food essential to the body; protein comes from meat, fish, eggs, cheese and milk. See also **carbohydrate, protein**.

quern Simple kind of mill, usually turned by hand; larger querns are turned by oxen or horses.

rancid Of butter, bad tasting and rotten.

reap To cut cereal crops at harvest time.

Roman empire Huge empire centred on Rome. It lasted from about 500 BC until AD 476. At its height it stretched from Scotland in the north to Egypt in the south and from Spain in the west to what is now Iraq in the east.

rye Cereal plant grown for its flour and for animal food; dried rye makes malt used to make whisky and other alcoholic drinks.

sheaf Bundle of grain plant tied together by the stalks.

sickle Short-handled curved knife that can be used with one hand to harvest crops.

staple The main food in a person's daily diet.

sterilize To heat to a high temperature to kill germs.

thresh To remove the grains of cereal plants from the stalks on which they grow.

veal Meat from young dairy cattle not wanted for milk production, usually young bulls.

vivarium In monasteries, a pond in which fish captured from rivers and lakes were kept alive until they were needed for the table.

wheat The world's most important cereal crop. It is grown for its flour to make bread and pasta and is also used to make many different kinds of breakfast cereal.

yeast Simple form of fungi. The yeast in bread changes the starch in the grain to sugar. The sugar breaks down into gas (carbon dioxide) and alcohol. The gas bubbles puff up the dough to make it rise.

INDEX

agora 24
American Civil war 40
amphorae 19
Appert, Nicolas 46
astronaut food 57
Aztecs 37

bacon 30
banana 45
Bakewell, Robert 50
Baltic sea 33
barley 15, 38; barley, wild 12-13
beans 15, 17, 24, 28, 29, 34
beekeeping 30
beer 21
Birdseye, Clarence 44
Black Death 32
bread making 20-1; bread, flat
  21; bread, raised 21
butter 30, 52

cabbage 17
can opener 47
carbohydrate 54-5, 60-1
cattle 10, 11, 15, 17, 38
cheese 11,17,18, 20, 24, 52
chickens 11, 17, 27
chilli pepper 35
clover 38
Columbus, Christopher 33, 35
combine harvester 40
cookshops 24
crop rotation 28, 38
curing meat 31

dehydration 57
diet 54-5
Drake, Sir Francis 36
drying meat 11, 30
Duroc pig 50

fallow fields 28, 32
famine 28
fat 54-5, 60-1
fertiliser 32, 48
fish 8,9,17, 46;
fishing boat 9; fishing industry
  58-9; fishing line 8; fishing
  nets 9
flail 15

freeze drying 56

garlic 15, 17
genetic engineering 60
goats 10, 11, 15, 17, 26, 27;
  goat's skin 11
grain 15, 20, 22-3, 28, 30
grapes 15, 17, 18, 19

Hampshire pig 50
herring 33
hoe 15
honey 17, 20, 24, 27, 30,37
hybrid plants and animals 60

ice box 45
ice cream 45
ice factory 45
Indians, American 5, 40
Inuit people 9
Irish potato famine 37

lard 11
leeks 187
Lent 33
lentils 15, 28
liquamen 24

maize 34, 35, 36, 37, 40; maize
  mill 37
maple syrup 41
markets 24
maslin 26
McCormick, Cyrus Hall 40
milk 11, 17, 20, 52-3; milk,
  condensed 53
mill 20, 28, 29, 39
monasteries 26-7
Moors 33,35
monoculture 36

Nile, River 14

olives 15, 17, 18, 19; olive groves
  16; olive oil 18, 19, 24
onions 15, 17, 26
oxen 6, 15, 29

SS Paraguay 45
Pasteur, Louis 52

pears 17
peas 17, 29
pedlars 24
pellagra 36
pepper 17, 20, 24, 30, 31
pig 11, 14, 26, 50
plough 15, 28, 29
Pompeii loaf 21
pork 15; pork, salt 26, 30
porridge 13, 21
potatoes 34,35 36;
potato beetle 37
potato blight 37
'potatom' 61
protein 54-5, 60-1

quern, rotary 20

radishes 15
Roman empire 16, 26-7
rye 27

salt 30
seed drill 38
shaduf 14

sheep, 10,11, 15, 17, 26, 27
sickle 15
slaves 35, 36
spices 16, 17, 19, 30; spices as
  digestive aid 30; spice trade 33
sugarcane 35
sweet pepper 34

terrace farming 48
three field system 28
Tull, Jethro 38
tomato 34, 35

vacuum packing 57
veal 50

watermill 29
windmill 39
wine 19, 22
wheat 15, 17, 22, 40

yeast 15, 20
Yorkshire pig 50

HOUSES

CLOTHES

COMMUNICATIONS

FOOD

TRANSPORT

TECHNOLOGY

   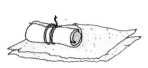